LIFE LESSONS FROM EZINNE VIRGINIA ADAEGO OGOKE-MY BELOVED MOTHER, MY REAL-LIFE HERO.

LIFE LESSONS FROM EZINNE VIRGINIA ADAEGO OGOKE-MY BELOVED MOTHER, MY REAL-LIFE HERO.

NGOZI D. MBUE

IngramSpark

This book is dedicated to my parents. Mom and Dad, I will always cherish your dedication to providing your family a better future. I am forever grateful for your sacrifices to give your children the best possible life. Thank you, Mom and Dad.

Library of Congress Cataloging-in-Publication Data
ISBN: 979-8-218-41677-5

First Printing, 2024

PROLOGUE

My mother significantly influenced me throughout my life, not because of what she did or said to me and my siblings but because of her extraordinary life. This is a woman whose husband passed away when she was in her 30s and who defied all odds and refused to remarry because she wanted to keep all her promises to her late husband. She dedicated her life to fighting for the things dear to her and her husband—a woman who ensured that her late husband's legacy continued even after their deaths. As a single mother, she raised five biological children and adopted five more children. Even though my mother did not have a formal education, she ensured that all her children received at least a high school education and excelled in whatever trade, profession, or training they pursued. She taught me that it does not matter where you come from or your circumstances in life but that trusting God and working hard will take you a long way. She taught me that it is not necessarily where you come from but where you are headed; what you have done or accomplished in life matters the most.

I became interested in authoring this memoir after my mother passed away. After talking to my siblings and my mother's relatives, I was inspired to write this book. I hope you will enjoy reading this book, filled with true stories and lessons I learned from the woman I call my beloved mother and my real-life hero.

CHAPTER 1

My Grandparents

My maternal grandfather's name was Korie Emetu, and he married my maternal grandmother, Anyaelesim-Lydia. My mother is from Ekwereazu, Ahiazu-Mbaise, Imo State, Nigeria. Ekwereazu is made up of six communities: Oparanadim, Mpam, Ihitteafoukwu, Umuokiriika, Obohia, and Ekwereazu Town. My mother's community is Ihitteafoukwu. My grandmother was a babysitter in my grandfather's compound in Ihitteafoukwu at an incredibly early age, probably under ten. While there, performing her duties, the family fell in love with her, and she later married my maternal grandfather. They were blessed with five children: a daughter named Ihuoma (a beautiful face), a son named Obilor Francis, my mother named Adaego Virginia, another daughter named Utemma Cecilia, and a son named Iwuji Cyracus.

I do not know much about my maternal grandfather. My mom told me that her father passed away when my mother was young. My mother thought highly of her father and would tell us stories about him in the most loving and passionate ways. My mother would say things about her father, such as, "I remember my dad so fondly." "He was strong and cared for his family the best he could."

My maternal grandmother did not have a formal education or training as a health care provider or professional. However, she was proficient in using local herbs to treat conditions such as menstrual cramps, seizures, constipation, and diarrhea. She also performed and perfected the act of delivering babies and helping women with fertility problems. My grandmother was not only a healer but also a prophetess and was well known for predicting events. She was well-loved and cherished in her community. Her husband died at a younger age, according to my mom, and my maternal grandmother raised her five young children as a single mother.

My maternal grandmother was a fantastic woman. She was always doing things and visiting places. Her extraordinary love for her children, grandchildren, great-grandchildren, and great-great-grandchildren was most notable. I was particularly fond of her and visited her every weekend throughout elementary school until she died in the 70s, around 1979. I remember her as a strong woman, and she refused to leave her house to live with any of her children and grandchildren; she lived at her own house until the day she passed away. While alive, she would visit her children and grandchildren periodically and then return to her house.

I remember the day my grandmother took her last breath like it was yesterday; I believe it was on a Friday evening in 1979. I was in elementary school then. My grandmother refused to live with any of her children as she got older. My mother and her sister (Utemma) would send us (My cousin Ahunna and me) all the food to take to our grandmother every Friday after school. My cousin and I always looked forward to visiting our grandmother every Friday. Upon arrival, my grandmother would cook all our special meals for us. We would perform all house chores, including fetching water from the stream, burning firewood, and going to our grandmother's farm with her. We always left every Sunday evening to go back home to get ready for school. On that particular Friday, our grandmother passed away; Ahunna and I arrived at her home to visit with her as usual, not knowing that would be our last moments with her. I remembered rushing towards and holding her as she sat on her bed with another neighbor. I will never forget the eye contact and the assurance on her face that everything would be okay. Immediately after she took her last breath, we heard a loud noise coming from her second bedroom. When we went outside, we saw that the wall had collapsed into tiny pieces while the rest of the building remained intact. Recently, I was with my cousin Ahunna, who was with me at the time of our grandmother's death, and she also recalled the collapse of the wall at the time of our grandmother's death. It was remarkable that the house was not destroyed even though a massive part of the walls collapsed.

What surprises and still baffles me today is how my maternal grandmother was able to prepare food for my cousin and me the day she died. There was nothing unusual on this day; after all, she always prepared food for us every weekend because she knew we were coming to visit. There was no indication that she was sick that week. Over the years, I contemplated what might have gone wrong but could not figure out why she had to pass away immediately after we got to her house.

Interestingly, she was able to prepare enough food that we ate for a couple of days until her funeral. I am so grateful that she waited for us to see her for the last time before she took her last breath. The memory of that day has stayed with me to this day and will probably remain so until my last day on Earth.

My maternal grandmother was a Christian and lived a simple and prayerful life. Being a servant of God was so important to her throughout her life. You could tell from how she went about her affairs as a testament to the woman she was. In her 90s, she indicated that she would like to be baptized. I remembered my mother's happiness when my grandmother hinted that she would like to be baptized. My mother prepared for the day of my grandmother's baptism by buying gifts for her and the priest. Father Oscar Fidelis Anyanwu, a Catholic priest in my grandmother's parish, was so kind to come to my grandmother's house for her baptism. At baptism, she was named Lydia Korie. After she was baptized, a significant and incredible holiness happened; my grandmother, in turn, also blessed Father Oscar and wished him well. I was not present during the baptismal ceremony, but how my mother described the whole event will stay with me forever. My mother described it as the most magical moment, filled with wonderment, love, and compassion. My mother indicated that she was mesmerized by my grandmother's blessing the priest afterward. Usually, when you visit a priest, you expect to receive a blessing from the priest and not vice versa. My mother said that the priest was grateful and delighted to receive his blessing from my grandmother.

My grandmother lived to be approximately 115-120 years old with over 100 grandchildren, great-grandchildren, and great-great-grandchildren before passing away in 1979. My grandmother did not have a birth certificate when she was born. She kept track of her age and the number of grandchildren, great-grandchildren, and great-great-grandchildren by collecting local beads and placing them on a string. She had a separate string of beads for her birthdays and another for when her grand or great-grandchildren gave birth. Over the years, these beads were made into necklaces. I was always elated each time I saw and touched those beads; they were so heavy and had beautiful colors; most of them were red. I remember wearing one of the beads around my neck during my visits with my grandmother. I was amazed at how heavy those beads felt around my neck.

My Beautiful Grandma Lydia

CHAPTER 2

My Young Mother

My mother was the third child of five siblings. As a child, my mother was greatly loved by everyone who met her. Many people described her as "very beautiful, caring, exceptionally honest, decent, honorable, respectful, never discriminated, and amiable." She wanted to get a formal education when she was growing up, but it was impossible because, at the time, there were no elementary schools in her hometown. There were a couple of elementary schools in nearby villages; however, it took about three to four hours from her house to get to school. One school close to my mother's hometown was St Joseph's Catholic School in Amakohia Ihitte; the school was more than three hours away. Interestingly, this school was in my hometown; my dad and I graduated from this elementary school. Other nearby schools were St. Augustine School in Oguri Mbano, more than three hours away, St. Columba in Nsu; Mbano, and St. Bridget's School in Ahiara, all at least three hours away from my maternal home.

Another reason that my mother did not go to school, as she would tell us, was because, growing up a beautiful girl, her family feared she might get kidnapped if she went to school far away. Another story my mother shared about not getting a formal education was due to one of the villagers whose daughter had a formal education but was unsure what level of education she was. When she got married, her bride price (a dowry paid to the girl's parents) was not much compared to the money the family spent putting her through school, and as a result, her father pleaded with the entire village not to send their daughters to school. If I remember correctly, my mother indicated she was already in elementary school with her younger sister Utemma, possibly in third grade. As a result, most parents in the neighborhood had to withdraw their daughters from school.

My mother was trained as a petty trader. She became interested in selling palm oil (used in cooking food). She became proficient in trading and traveled to markets in surrounding villages with her younger sister Utemma, who was selling fish then. In addition, my mother enjoyed farm work and would help her mother farm in her various gardens. She once told us that her young sister Utemma enjoyed cooking and detested farming. Sometimes, when they would go to the farm, my Auntie Utemma would make an excuse to go back home to prepare meals before my mom returned from the farm.

Another passion of my mother's was dancing. She participated in the local dance that usually took place on special market days. There was a dance called "Nwakorobo" in which young girls like my mother would participate on market days. As they danced, potential suitors would come from nearby villages to witness these young ladies dancing. At the end of each dance, any potential suitor who saw the dance would approach the girl he was interested in, follow her home, and propose. I was told it was during one of those times that my father met my mother and became interested in her.

Another story that remains vivid in my memory is one that my mother told us countless times: the times my dad would visit their village and the reactions of the village people each time he visited, wearing his army uniforms and riding his famous bicycle. My mother said that some of the villagers who saw them together would feel sorry for her and make gestures that depicted torture and suffering. The assumption was that when you marry a soldier, he is bound to beat you up because of the nature of his military training. My mother told us that some of the signs were hilarious and that she and my dad would laugh at those people and some of their signs. It was funny because my dad was not a violent man. But those people were basing their assumptions on the fact that my dad was wearing an army uniform. My mother said that sometimes my dad would tell her not to listen to those people because she would sometimes buy into their assumptions and innuendos. I miss listening to my mother telling us these stories. I laughed hard whenever my mother told us about all these people and their beliefs.

My mother (extreme right) with her sisters
Auntie Utemma (extreme left) and Nene
Ihuoma (eldest sister) in the middle.

CHAPTER 3

My Dad and His Family

According to my dad's diary entries, he was born in 1922. His full name was Columba Ejiniemekaibe Ogoke. He was nicknamed "Okokpaikpai" because of his swiftness and urgency in handling his affairs. He started elementary school in 1932. My dad passed Standard VI (probably the equivalent of 12th grade) in 1941 at St. Joseph's Catholic School, my alma mater. He was so happy that he wrote in his diary, "My last trouble in school." My dad left home for Zaria on April 24th, 1942, a metropolitan city in Nigeria. In September of the same year, he indicated that he was forced to join the Second World War to fight for the British since Nigeria was a British colony. While serving in the army in October 1943, he met and married our mother. In 1945, he was promoted to Corporal in a ceremony officiated by Captain Allen. On May 25th, 1945, my dad was promoted to first-class Storekeeper. Nigeria remained a colony under British rule until it gained independence on October 1st, 1960. As mentioned above, my dad fought in the Second World War under the British Army, stationed in Djibouti. Djibouti is officially called the Republic of Djibouti; it is a small country in the Horn of Africa, bordered by Somalia in the south, Ethiopia in the southwest, Eritrea in the north, and the Red Sea and the Gulf of Aden in the east. On February 28th, 1947, my dad was honorably discharged from the army. On March 10th, 1947, he left Zaria for his hometown in Amakohia-Ihitte in the former Etiti Local government, Imo State-Nigeria.

My dad passed away at an incredibly young age. He was barely 40 years old when he passed away. I came to know my dad through my conversations with my mother, siblings, family friends, and acquaintances of my dad and my dreams of him. This may sound weird. Throughout elementary school, I saw my dad in my dreams. He would appear mainly at the head of my bed and look down at me. He was tall, handsome, dark-skinned, and slim. He would wear white outfits, just like what a priest in the Catholic Church would wear. He mostly came when I needed him the most, for example, during big celebrations such as Christmas, New Year's, and Easter. Growing up as kids, we would shop and buy primarily clothes, shoes, and handbags instead of toys during Christmas or special occasions, unlike how it is done in the Western world. As a child, I would listen to my friends tell me how they would go to the stores and malls with their dads to buy some of their gifts. I often felt lonely and would miss my dad at that moment. In my dreams, my dad would usually appear and take me places, including shopping centers. I would've wanted to go with him in real life. I felt close to my dad when I was growing up. In my dreams, he was patient with me, waiting until I recognized him as he stood by the head of my bed for a while most nights. I felt I had gotten to know him; he was there every night in my dreams when I needed him. It was such a calm and loving experience to have him around in my dreams growing up. I will always be grateful to him for reaching out to me in such a unique manner.

My dad was born a Prince. His dad was an Eze (King in the Igbo language) and a ruler who helped bring Christianity to our area. When the missionaries came to my village, I was told that my grandfather welcomed them and gave them land to build schools, a catholic seminary (where young boys are trained to become priests), and a church where the villagers worshipped. My family continued to provide land to the church whenever they needed to expand the church or the seminary. I know that growing up, we had a lot of landed property and resources. Most of the landed properties in my village were once owned by my family before they were either sold or offered as a gift to another family in my town. One of my late uncles told me my grandfather married approximately 33 women. Most of the women and the lands were given to him by families who could not afford to pay him for his services to them. One such service was settling family cases for people in court. I commended my paternal grandfather for providing for all his wives. Each household member was allotted properties and resources handed down to generations. I still marvel at how my grandfather could care for all his family members and their generations afterward.

Reading my dad's diary, I found out that my grandfather passed away around 1946-1947. My dad indicated around April 30th, 1947, that he had contacted the most senior brother (Nnawuihe Ogoke) several times to meet with him so that they could go over their father's affairs and the burial expenses. It appeared that his senior brother stonewalled him and seemed uninterested in meeting him initially, and I could not tell from his diary when he finally met with his brothers.

Based on my relatives' stories, my dad was one of my paternal grandfather's most beloved sons. He was his mother's only child; she passed away when my dad was young. Another woman named Ugodi raised my dad as her own child, along with another stepson named Ifeanyichukwu, whom my dad loved so much and treated as his younger brother. I was lucky to come in contact with my dad's diary in 2010 when I visited home with my whole family for the first time, and my mom was made Ezinne in the Catholic Church. Ezinne or Nneoma titles are merit awards given to women of great honor or integrity. Celebrating these titles is common in the Catholic church and other Christian denominations. The titles are bestowed on mothers who are grounded in knowledge of the church and family and are respected for their long-standing experiences in matters of human wisdom and judgment. Recipients must have demonstrated their faith, morals, and ethics in the Catholic Church and the community. Before this trip, I had always visited my mom and relatives in Nigeria alone. One of my uncles kept this diary for all those years, and it was in bad shape when he gave it to me. I could not help but think why he did not give my family our dad's diary over the years since his death.

My dad married my mom in 1943 while still in the army. In 1944, they were blessed with a daughter named Catherine Ada, who passed away in 1946 in Zaria. Then, another daughter, Rosaline (fondly called Daa Rose) Chinuruoka, was born on November 11th, 1946. Another daughter, Bernadette Uluoma, was born on April 19th, 1949, and passed away on May 30th, 1953, when my mom and the kids traveled to the village; then a son, whom my dad named Prince Charles Ahamefule, was born on March 6th, 1952. Unfortunately, on January 9th, 1954, Charles passed away when my mom visited our hometown with the kids. Another daughter, Bibiana Chinwe, was born on May 28th, 1954; a daughter named Cordelia Uzoamaka was born in 1957. My Dad's official last entry in his diary was in 1957. I have always wondered why my dad no longer made entries in his diary after 1957. I did not see any information about my immediate elder sister Fidelia Obiageri's (fondly called Daa Oby) birth information or any information about my birth in my Dad's diary. My sister, Daa Oby, was born in October 1960 when Nigeria became independent. Growing up, Daa Oby always alluded to the fact that she was born during Nigeria's independence. I know I was born before the Nigerian-Biafran War in 1967. I always remember how one of my sisters, Bibianna, narrated how difficult it was to carry me around during the war.

My parents had their share of pain and losses. I was told two other sons died before I was born after my sister Obiageri (Daa Oby), and they lost their beloved Catherine, Bernadette, and Charles at young ages. I could only imagine my parents' anguish after losing so many children. "Oh, death, what I have done to you, please," my dad wrote in his diary. I have three living biological siblings from my parents and five siblings whom my mother adopted. In December 2022, we lost one of my siblings, Fidelia Obiageri (fondly called Daa Oby) Amaechi—a terrible loss to our family. I am still struggling to reconcile the circumstances leading to her death and the pain she endured those months before she died.

My father left the army in 1947 and got a job with the Federal Railway Corporation as a head guard. He worked in many places in northern Nigeria. He worked in Zaira in Kaduna state in Nigeria, where my sisters Rose and Catherine were born. He was later transferred to Maiduguri and Otukpo in Benue, Nigeria. Since living in these areas, both parents became proficient in the native languages and the Hausa language. All my siblings were born out of state, except for my sister Bibianna; we called her Daa Baby when my mother visited home. My dad was later transferred to Port-Harcourt, the last place we lived before his death and my birthplace.

My dad worked hard. He loved his children so much. He referred to my mother in his diary as "My Sweetheart Mrs." My parents shared a bond that would never be broken. My parents were both lovers of education. My mother would tell us my dad's last wishes to her included taking loving care of his children and making sure his children got an education, among others. As a child, I realized that getting a formal education was important to my dad and mother. It became essential to me to get an education as I was growing up. The quest to get an education made me, over the years, keep reaching higher and getting to the utmost level of degree possible- a PhD. To me, embracing and excelling in my studies was a way to honor my dad's and my mother's wishes and aspirations.

My Dad, this is the only picture that I have of
him.

CHAPTER 4

Our Beautiful Historic House and Circumstances Leading to My Dad's Death

Unfortunately, my dad was poisoned when he arrived home to arrange for our brand-new open-house ceremony. Our beautiful and historic home was our dad's last gift to my family. Our house was situated on a beautiful and strategic place, a federal road that would lead to most cities around my area. A beautiful house in the 1960s was named "A Little House of No Regret" by my dad—the first of its kind in the 1960s. I was told the whole town went wild when the house was completed within six months and how beautiful it looked inside and outside, with roses, plants, and trees around it—a four-bedroom house with a central parlor or sitting area for visitors. The house also had a beautiful, covered patio big enough to seat many people. The bathroom and the toilet were constructed outside the bedrooms. The backyard has ample space, and another two rooms inside the backyard serve as a kitchen and storage area. A tall fence made of bricks and barbed wire on top was around the house for protection, making it hard for anyone to sneak inside our house without being caught. And doors were in the

front and backyard. The backyard gate led to the neighbors who lived
behind us. Growing up, I always liked how I could sneak out of the
backyard to visit my friends without anyone noticing that I was gone. I
always felt safe inside our house. Even now, when I visit our house, I always feel safe. My mother told us there was a lot of interest in the house
from the villagers and my dad's brothers while it was being constructed.
It was a historic house and an essential landmark. Our home also had
plants, oranges, tangerines, mango trees, guava, cashew trees, cherry
trees, and roses everywhere. I always enjoyed eating the fruits from all
these trees. Without climbing the trees, I would reach for the tangerine
and the cashews. Everybody who grew up in my town knows my house.
Married couples used to go there and take their wedding photos. People
would choose to meet each other there for a meeting. I loved that house,
one of only two modern homes around my area at the time. I was told
there was only one modern house with a close resemblance to our house
at that time, not too far from ours. The most haunting and emotional
fact about our house was that my father never slept in that house while
he was alive. He was laid in state briefly when he passed away. Until
the day my mother passed away, she never stopped talking about how it
broke her heart that my dad never slept in our house while he was alive.
My mother told the story that the initial plan was to build our house in
Port-Harcourt, where we lived. Following this, my mother advised my
dad to build a small house in the village first so that we would have a
place to stay when we visited home instead of sharing my grandpa's big
house with all my dad's siblings. Our house was probably the last gift
from my dad to my mother and all of us.

My mother always appreciated having a place to stay when we
finally came home after our dad passed away. It never came easy because
immediately after my dad passed away, some of my uncles moved inside
the house and started claiming ownership and sending us away. My
mother fought hard for us to move into our house. One of my sisters
told me that we almost did not move in. We had to move in at night to
avoid alerting my evil uncles, who wanted the house. I was told one of
my uncles had already entertained his guests at our house and was also

using our house as his rest house before we finally moved in and settled in our house.

My elder sister, Rosaline, was young when our dad passed away. She said that she had visited home with our dad when he was poisoned and that dad had gone out with his siblings to celebrate and plan for the opening of our brand-new house. Our very generous dad was planning a big celebration that would include all the women married to my grandfather, including their children and relatives. He planned to provide wrappers for uniforms and food to be cooked for all and invite several people within the village, from the towns and nearby villages, for the ceremony.

While my dad was out, he bought drinks and other things for his brothers. It was during this time that his drink was poisoned. My sister indicated they were supposed to return to Port Harcourt the next day when our dad started getting sick. At that time, the means of transportation was by train. While inside the train, my dad mainly threw up dark and bloody vomit. My sister described it as the worst experience of her life, just watching our dad being sick and gradually losing his strength. When they arrived in Port Harcourt, my dad was not doing well. My mother said he told her when they finally arrived that he had prayed to God to spare him time to see his wife and his children again before joining his ancestors. Thankfully, he did get to see my mother and his children before he was taken to the hospital and received last rites from the priest before he passed away. Ironically, some of my dad's brothers who planned and killed him bragged about their evil acts after my dad died. Over the years, we realized it was out of jealousy of the fact that my dad worked hard and was more industrious than his siblings. My dad worked hard for everything he achieved in his short life and was generous with his time and wealth. After our mother's memorial service, I visited my elder sister (Rose) before returning to the United States. She said this about our dad: "Papa was dark, handsome, huge, and tall. Papa was kind. He bought things for people and was a humanitarian." My sister, who was probably 12 years old, then indicated she was traumatized to see our dad getting so sick and helpless on the train back to Port

Harcourt. She said our dad initially played his ill health off and did not want to alarm her. Not surprisingly, I was told that he was naturally pleasant, caring, and loving to everyone he met. He reassured our sister that nothing would happen to him when he got sick. My sister said that our dad masking how sick he was initially made her feel at ease, and he even tried to play with her as he continued to throw up and felt sick.

At that time, my sister Rose indicated that because our dad worked with the Federal Railway, they always took first class, which was more accessible, faster, and most means of transportation. As they returned to Port Harcourt by train, all the passengers and some of my dad's co-workers were also alarmed and scared for my dad. In his usual ways, my dad tried to calm everyone down and told them he was not sick. My sister said he was more concerned about the plight of everyone else inside the train than himself and remained optimistic and cheerful as he lay there so sick. My sister said she had not forgotten that experience and how courageous our dad was even as he lay down so ill and nearing death.

My Dad's Diary. One of my uncles had this
diary all these years. It was given to my family
in 2010. It was not kept in good condition.

Now, A Little of No Regret. This is a section of
the house-our Dad's last gift to us. This is not
how I remember our house growing up. Inside
are some of my parent's grandkids.

CHAPTER 5

Diobu, Where My Father Lived in Port Harcourt

Diobu is a densely populated neighborhood located within the Port Harcourt metropolis. Port Harcourt is the capital and largest city in Rivers State, Nigeria. It is Nigeria's fifth most populous city after Lagos, Kano, Ibadan, and Benin. I was told that the area that became Port Harcourt around 1912 was part of the farmland of the Indigenous people of Rebisi (Ikwere). The colonial administration of Nigeria created the port to export coal from the collieries of Enugu, located about 151 miles north of Port Harcourt. Port Harcourt's economy turned to petroleum when the first shipment of Nigerian crude oil was exported through the city around 1958. Through the benefits of the Nigerian petroleum industry, Port Harcourt was further developed, with the city having overpasses and more modern infrastructure. Most oil firms, including Shell and Chevron, have offices in Port Harcourt.

My parents settled in Diobu before the Nigerian-Biafra war. This place was crucial to my dad's job. Diobu consists of three main extensions: Mile One, Mile Two, and Mile Three markets. Most of the commercial activities in Diobu exist in its numerous markets. Present-day Diobu ranks highly among the most commercially vibrant places in the city, attracting talented professionals such as soccer players and other talents in science and technology.

Many people, especially the Igbos, settled here because of the business and commercial opportunities. Many Igbo people fled the city when the war broke out, abandoning their homes and valuables. Some of the remaining people were killed by the troops and non-Igbo residents. I was told that there were some aspects of other ethnic groups that welcomed the arrival of the Nigerian troops and laid claim to some of the vacated properties and filled local leadership positions. After the war, some Igbo community members returned to Port Harcourt and salvaged whatever they could of their abandoned properties. My family was not able to go back to Port Harcourt. I was told that one of my uncles could return to work at the Railway in my Dad's place. My mom told us that after my dad passed away, the company suggested that a family member work in the place of my dad to help raise his young children. My mother recommended one of my uncles named Ifeanyichukwu, whom my dad brought up and referred to as his younger brother. This particular uncle never cared about my mother or siblings growing up, disappointing my mother and us. My mom always regretted sending this uncle to represent my dad. My mom thought she was doing a good thing to have my uncle represent my dad and my family, and it turned out to be one of the decisions my mom regretted until she passed away. It would have been helpful if this uncle had been in our lives growing up.

CHAPTER 6

The Impact of the Nigerian -Biafra War

To my mother, the civil war in Nigeria was another unforgettable time for her after our dad's death. Nigeria got her independence from the British government in 1960. A couple of years later, it was said that there was turmoil in northern Nigeria, where some Christian Igbos did not have a good relationship with the Hausas, who were predominantly Muslim. The beauty of Nigeria is the blessing of the existence of many ethnic groups, cultures, and dialects. The Igbos felt unprotected and established the Republic of Biafra under the leadership of Lieutenant Colonel Odumegwu Ojukwu and other non-Igbo representatives. After diplomatic efforts to reunite the country failed, a civil war broke out between Nigeria and Biafra in 1967. My dad passed away shortly before this time, and we lived in Port Harcourt, where I was born. My mother did her best to raise her five children by herself, and as a family, we were okay.

The war seemed to be lingering; initially, many people were unaffected. Under the leadership of Ojukwu, Biafra made some headway but could not do so much because of Nigeria's superior military strength, which gradually reduced Biafra's territory. The worst impact on Biafra was losing its oil fields, one of the primary sources of revenue, and limited funds to import foods. Millions died due to malnutrition and other war-related incidences. The war lasted for approximately three years, from 1967 to 1970. In January 1970, Nigerian forces captured

Owerri, one of the Biafra strongholds, which led to Ojukwu fleeing to Ivory Coast, a neighboring country to Nigeria. Not too long after Ojukwu left the country, Biafra surrendered to Nigeria.

As the war was going on, we were forced to return home and lost most of our belongings in Port Harcourt, just like everyone who fled because of the war. My mother would tell the story that the officials at the federal railway where my dad worked and where my uncle was working during the war provided my family support through my uncle to make sure all our things were being transported to our house in the suburbs. This would have aided my uncle in transporting us back to our house with all our belongings intact. Instead, my uncle did not help us as directed but helped transport all his in-law's belongings to their house. My mother was so disappointed and would tell us about the belongings we lost in Port Harcourt during the war—all of my dad's belongings, including house items such as expensive dishes and all household items, that my dad spent a lot of time acquiring while alive.

I was told we stayed at my maternal home during the war, inside the suburbs of a nearby village in my town. There, we had hiding areas that sheltered people during the day and sometimes at night when the airplanes would parade the areas, killing people and destroying properties.

My mother fought hard to maintain our brand-new house, which was pretty new; when the war started, my mother did not want anything happening to the house or thieves stealing things from our house. My mother would, in the evenings while we were at my maternal home, return to spend the night with one of my siblings and to make sure nothing happened to our house or any of the things inside the one. A tenant living at our home then fled with his family. My mother was concerned that nothing would happen to their belongings and risked her life and would return to our house to spend the night.

After the war, the Nigerian soldiers occupied our house and used it as one of their offices and living headquarters. We could not return to our house right away after the war. But my mother, fluent in the Hausa language, managed to convince the soldiers, who mostly spoke it, that they needed to pay us rent, and they did as my mother requested. When

I heard this story, I could not fathom how my mom managed to pull this off, having the soldiers pay her rent as they forcefully occupied the house.

After a while, the soldiers were asked to return to the barracks, and we were allowed to return to our house. After the war, many things changed. The currency is now Nigerian currency. When he was alive, my dad worked hard and saved most of his money in Biafra currency. My mother tried to recover some of my dad's money from the bank, but she was not that successful, and she never stopped remembering and discussing the loss during and after the war. She felt that was another trying moment after our dad passed away.

CHAPTER 7

Married Life and Difficulties Faced After My Dad Died

My mother was in her thirties when our dad passed away. Now, with five surviving children and no job or enough money, my mother decided she would devote her life to her children and would not remarry, even with all the suitors interested in marrying her. She said, "My husband and I loved each other so much. I will not marry again." Not too long after my dad passed away, we were forced to leave Port Harcourt and return to the village because of the Nigerian-Biafra war.

My mother often alluded to the fact that she lost most of our belongings during the war because we were forced to leave most things behind. Most tragically, the currency was changed after the war, and my mother could not recover all the money my dad had saved in the bank. The pound (symbol £) was the currency of the breakaway Republic of Biafra between 1968 and 1970. The Republic of Biafra, under the Biafran President Colonel Odumegwu Ojukwu, existed from 1967 to 1970 as an independent state between Nigeria and Cameroon. My mother would periodically say that the war cost her a lot and was the next terrible and tragic event after losing our dad.

After the war, it became increasingly difficult for my mother to raise her children. Now, we were forced to return to our home in the suburbs. After my dad passed away, my mother recommended that one of my uncles be hired by my dad's railway company. The notion was for

him to take care of us as he continued to work for the Railway, but this
never happened. Our lives became hell immediately after my dad passed
away and when we returned home. As you would expect from a large
family, some of my uncles were not nice to us. First, it was a miracle
that we could move into our brand-new home, as some of my uncles
attempted to stop us from moving in. My mother fought hard for us
to move in. One of my siblings told me we had to quietly move to our
house at nighttime by God's grace. While living at our home, we were
constantly being threatened. Some of my uncles resorted to claiming
everything that belonged to our dad. Even before my mother could visit
the bank after my dad passed away to claim some of my dad's money in
his bank account, one of my uncles had already taken another woman
who posed as my mother to claim my dad's money. Another one of my
evil uncles threatened to kill my mother, which warranted my maternal
grandmother and my mother's siblings intervening and warning them
to stay away from my mother and all of us.

Too many threats were being leveled consistently at my mother by
some of my evil uncles. I remember at least four evil uncles who went
too extreme with their treats, stole some of my dad's landed properties,
and profited from them. My mother remained steadfast through it all
and would not let any of those bother her. I remember that on so many
occasions, I remember at least one of my evil uncles stealing our lands
and resources and selling them without consulting or giving any money
to my mother. Even over the years, I remember a particular son of one
of the uncles continuing on his father's evil ways and stealing our land
and some other properties from us. My mother would often fight off
some of my greedy uncles, and sometimes, she was unsuccessful. An
overwhelming assumption by some of my uncles was that my mother
now only had females and no male child to represent and keep my
dad's lineage. My mother should remarry, hence the unending harass-
ment and maltreatment. One thing that stood out for me as a child
throughout those periods was my mother's unwavering faith in God.
My mother might have sometimes felt disappointed with the actions of
my evil uncles, but she never showed any animosity toward my wicked

uncles, who were mean and abusive to her. My mother treated all of them with respect and was never bitter or showed any sign of ill feelings towards them. My mother was always present and supported them, their wives, and their children in everything they did, which to this day amazes me.

I remember on specific occasions when we cooked special meals or meats, and my mother would send my siblings or myself to deliver part of the food or meat to my uncles. I remember a couple of times when we would prepare chicken to celebrate special occasions; my mother sent the gizzards to my uncles. My mother believed men should eat the gizzards, not the women. On special events, I was sent by my mother to deliver certain foods or meats to my uncles; the thought crossed my mind to eat some of the food or even eat all of it on my way to my uncles. But when I thought of how my mother would feel, I restrained myself and never carried out my plan. Sometimes, I felt mad and argued with my mother that my wicked uncles did not deserve respect or any food my mother had offered to my evil uncles.

CHAPTER 8

My Mom as She Raised Her Children

My mother initially could not understand how my beloved dad could die just like that after visiting his home and his brothers. Initially, my mother did not know how to move on when our dad died. She would say that looking at us brought her joy and would propel her to keep fighting. My mother said that while our dad was alive, he would not let her do much at home. Throughout their marriage, my dad sent all his clothes to the cleaners, except his underwear, which my mother would wash at home. They had servants and housekeepers, including family members who were always available to help in the house. My dad was generous, paid the school fees for many people, and trained his siblings in various trades. My parents were considered one of the wealthiest couples in my village then, mainly because they had the ability and the money to build our brand-new house within six months, which was not common in the sixties in my town. Another thing was the ability of my parents to help care for and assist relatives from both my mother's and Dad's homes. In my dad's diary, I saw where he documented the names of friends and family members to whom he lent money and the landed properties and resources he purchased.

Now living at our brand-new house, with no formal education and less money, my mother resorted to using her previous experience in petty trading to embark on trading and exporting palm oil from our town to big cities like Lagos. She became a successful entrepreneur. She would travel to Lagos with large drums of palm oil and sell them and bring other things to sell at home before she traveled to Lagos again. When she was not traveling, she would sew clothes at the local market. I enjoyed going to the market with her as I got older because I knew she would buy me treats. I do not remember my family going without food any day. I realized that when things got tough sometimes, and my mom did not have enough food for us, she would decide not to eat so that we could have enough to eat. My favorite days of the week were Wednesdays, Fridays, and Sundays because those were the days we ate rice and beans along with goat meat and fresh fish, my favorite foods growing up. My mother also liked to farm and plant all kinds of produce, harvest them, and sell them at the market. I became so interested in whatever she did and sometimes went to the farm with her.

As we started school, it became increasingly difficult for my mother to pay all the school fees and feed us. One of my uncles in the 1970s was exceptional and helped my mother in the littlest ways he could. Not long afterward, my uncle died in a terrible accident, another blow to my family. I remember how benevolent this particular uncle, Papa Amah, was. He helped my mom pay for our school fees. I still remember a special box made locally that my uncle purchased for my siblings for their school supplies. We called those locally made boxes Tinkers. Anyone who attended elementary school in the 1970s or 1980s probably used one of these boxes. They are so durable that they prevent school supplies or books from getting destroyed when it rains. I remember using one of the boxes my sisters gifted me in elementary school. It was such a memorable experience.

My adorable late uncle participated in constructing a big market center (Ariaria International Market). The Ariaria International Market is an open-air market located in Abia, a city in Abia State in southeast Nigeria. The market is one of the largest markets in West Africa, nicknamed the "China of Africa" because of its versatility in making wear and leather works. While riding one of the giant bulldozers (powerful tractors), my late uncle was involved in a terrible accident and was taken to the hospital, where he died. One of the trees he was trying to uproot fell on top of him and caused severe harm to him.

Still, through it all, my mother did ensure that we all got an education. I became so interested in learning as soon as I could start school, which initially took much work to get me to school. As a child, I never wanted to leave my mom's presence. I needed to be around and protect her, even as a kid. I will not forget my mother's support, especially when she realized my interest in attending college and pursuing further education. On so many occasions, my mother would trade her wrapper or personal jewelry as collateral to get enough money to pay our school fees. One of my uncles paid my tuition and boarding school fees for my first year in high school. When I was getting ready to go back for my sophomore year, I went to my uncle for my school fees, and he told me right at his house that he could not support my education anymore. That was my uncle, whom my dad helped by paying for his education; by then, he was a school principal. I remember coming home so distraught and scared that I would not be able to go back to school. My mother consoled me and promised to do everything she could to ensure I returned to school. I could feel the agony and the fear in her voice, which she meticulously hid from me. I was so happy when I could return to school with the help of one of my sisters (Daa Baby), who started working by then, and I have not been able to forget that moment to this day.

My mother never wavered in supporting her children's education, especially my pursuits. In elementary school, my mother encouraged me to reach for the stars. While in elementary school, every Monday morning, I would recite a couple of passages from the Bible in front of the school audience. Seeing my mother smiling and happy for me was always a joy. She would remind us often to do our homework. She would tell us stories from the Bible, though she could not read, primarily stories told to her as she was growing up and during church activities. Some of my favorite moments were when we would go home with our end-of-year progress report cards. My mother would ask if I came first in class. Watching her dance and being happy yearly gave me joy when I told her my grade. Seeing how happy she was as I did well at school was one of the reasons I became so interested in getting under-graduate and graduate education. I will never forget when I defended my dissertation while getting my PhD. I called my mother and told her I just defended my dissertation, and she said, "My daughter, you have made your dad and myself proud today. You have succeeded in fulfilling one of your dad's last wishes. I am so proud of you."

My mother ensured we attended church every Sunday and other days of obligation. She was tough and would not let my sisters be around boys, even visiting potential suitors before marriage. She would frown at the idea of us spending time alone with any boy. My mother attended morning church services and recited Holy Rosary every day as far back as I could remember. She was instrumental in my knowing God early on. I remember at a younger age, possibly five years old, waking up at 4:30 am most days to attend morning church service and Holy Rosary before going to school. We would walk down to St. Joseph's Catholic Church and School every morning with our lanterns as there were no streetlights then. We would be reciting the Holy Rosary on our way to church and would complete all the decades before arriving there. For Catholics, reciting the Holy Rosary is essential to our faith. The Holy Rosary has 59 beads, a crucifix, and a medal, with specific prayers for each piece. The prayers of the Holy Rosary can be divided into three categories (Introductory Prayers, The Decades, and the Closing Pray-ers). The Hail Mary prayer is the heart of the Holy Rosary. We pray 10 Hail Mary's within each of the five decades-totaling 50 Hail Mary pray-ers at the end of each devotion, including the three Hail Mary's Prayer at the Introductory Prayers (a total of 53 Hail Mary Prayers). When praying the Holy Rosary, we ask Mary, the mother of Jesus, to pray for us and guide us by the example of Her son, Jesus. The Holy Rosary is a Scripture-based prayer that leads us to Jesus through His mother, Mary. Mother Mary, also known as the Lady of Rosary, urged everyone to pray the Holy Rosary to help people grow in their faith, convert sinners, and bring world peace. On the days that I had to stay back and sweep the church, as we used the same building for the school, my mother would ensure I had breakfast and warm water to bathe by the time I got home. On Sundays after morning mass, we would return to the church in the evenings for Benediction, which I immensely enjoyed. She encouraged us to help clean the church on weekends, belong to various religious organizations, go for periodic reconciliations, and receive Holy Communion.

Our mom on the day she was made Ezinne.

My mom, my family, and the priest, after my mom was made Ezinne in the Catholic church.

With most of my siblings, when my mom was made Ezinne in the Catholic church.

I read my mom's biography during the Ezinne ceremony with my other three sisters (Daa Oby, Daa Rose, and Daa Cordy).

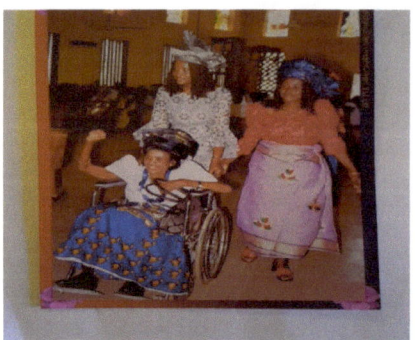

With my mom, my sister Obiageri-fondly called Daa Oby-Rest in Peace!

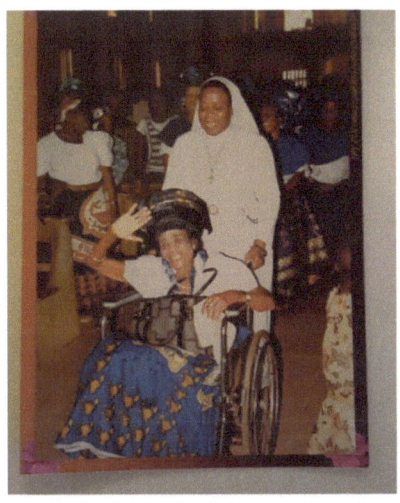

My mom was with one of the nuns, a good
family friend. Mom was so happy.

My mom thanked everyone during the Ezinne
ceremony. My brother was in the middle
behind my mom.

My mom, with members of the Ezinne present
during the ceremony.

During the Ezinne ceremony with my family. It
was such a joyous occasion for everyone.

With John during the Ezinne ceremony.

CHAPTER 9

My Mom's Passion

My mother enjoyed praying a lot, among other things. My mom recited the Holy Rosary every day. In later years, she would say the Rosary more than once daily. Another passion of hers was attending church service every day and days of obligation. She would wake up as early as four to attend morning mass or church service. On the way, she would recite the Rosary as she walked towards the church building. Usually, a Rosary would be said before the mass, and my mother would ensure she participated in the Rosary and sometimes led the Rosary sessions.

My mom enjoyed Latin Mass. Though she had no formal education, she could follow up in Latin whenever the priest conducted mass in Latin. She belonged to so many religious organizations. She was the head of women's organizations in my extended family. She was the driving force in ensuring everyone in my big compound performed their duties to the church and the community. My mom was active in church, had done lots of volunteer work there, and was beloved by all in the community. In 2010, she was made an Ezinne (a great mother) in church, an honor given to a few women in the Catholic Church and other religious organizations.

Another passion of my mother was her dedication to her grand and great-grandchildren. She was devoted to raising her children despite her extreme hardships. She commented numerous times that raising her children was one of the good things she did in life. How she raised her children depicted her love and respect for her late husband. Later in life, my mother adopted five more children as we grew older. She made sure everyone got at least a high school education. She particularly liked all her adopted children, especially my brother Chimaobi, whom she fondly called CC and regarded as the head of the household.

My mother also loved her farming in our various gardens. She grew much produce, more than enough for the household, and some left-overs she would sell at the market and donate to others less privileged than us. I remember sometimes helping her take things to the market to sell and helping send things to other people in the village. She made sure that our father's land and other resources were protected. She could have sold some of the land to raise money for us, but instead, she cultivated the land and planted crops to make money and to give to other people.

Trading and sewing clothes for people were among the things that my mother enjoyed doing. She would travel to Lagos and nearby local markets to sell items at the store. Sometimes, when I was at the local market with my mother, and she wanted to buy food, she would buy one of the inexpensive food items to save enough to buy food for us. Some of the women in our village would come to my mom for training on buying and selling palm oil. I remember one of the tenants at our house was interested in buying and selling palm oil; my mother trained her and helped start her own trading business. My mother would sew clothes at the market whenever she was not buying or trading palm oil. She would make people's clothes and only take a little money from them.

With some of the grandkids during one of my visits to Nigeria. Picture taken inside our family home.

Picture with some of my parents' grandkids after a church service
during one of my visits to Nigeria.

With beautiful Chinyere, my parents' first grandchild. One of my best
friends!!

Another picture with grandkids.

Another picture with beautiful Chinyere.

CHAPTER 10

My Mom Visit to the United States

My mother visited the United States in June 1999, when I had my first child (Mojo). My husband and I invited her to spend time with us and her new granddaughter. It was quite an experience for my mother. Living in the United States, she experienced a severe culture shock. It was intriguing to her that we had to lock the doors daily, even inside our apartment. She could not imagine why we had to do that. Growing up, we never had to close the doors of our house back in Nigeria. Our house is close to the federal road that leads to other cities. Anybody can practically walk right inside our house without prior notice. Sometimes, we saw weird folks walking inside our home asking for food. My mother welcomed everyone to our house.

My mother could not understand why we wore pants to church and did not cover our heads with a scarf. Initially, she would get mad at me for not covering my head or wearing pants to church. Another shock to her was receiving Holy Communion on both hands in church. Growing up, you always stuck your tongue out to receive Holy Communion and would be careful not to let Communion fall out of your mouth. But she enjoyed the English Mass, even the periodic Latin Mass. She always went to mass on Sundays or days of obligation.

While in the United States, my mother enjoyed meeting people from different ethnic groups and all walks of life. She would shake hands with strangers, even though she may not have understood their languages. We were living in Kansas City, Missouri when she visited us, and she especially enjoyed the outings and other Cameroonian and Nigerian functions we attended. My husband was born in Cameroon, but we met in the United States. My mom was fond of my husband and his culture. Initially, I was concerned whether my mom would be able to communicate with my husband as he is not fluent in my native dialect, the Igbo language. Still, to my surprise, my mom had a good relationship with my husband and interacted well with my husband. My mom could speak pidgin English. A pidgin language is a grammatically simplified means of communication that develops between two or more groups of people who do not have a language in common. Its vocabulary and grammar are limited and often drawn from several languages. In general, pidgin is not the native language of any community but is learned as a second language. A pidgin may be built from words, sounds, body language from many languages, and onomatopoeia. Onomatopoeia is using or creating a word that phonetically imitates, resembles, or suggests the described sound. You will be amazed to hear those without formal education speaking fluent pidgin. I was happy that my mom could communicate with my husband through pidgin.

My mom communicated with my husband well and was impressed with the care she received from my husband. When my mom visited, my husband and I were attending graduate school. During a break from classes, my husband would rush home to make lunch for my mom. Initially, my mom was scared of using the gas cooker and reluctant to warm food in the microwave. My husband would be home when I was at work or school to help prepare my mom's lunch. My mom bonded with my husband over this gesture. My mom was impressed with my husband and would sometimes allude to me that I should be the one who was supposed to come home and make lunch for her, not my husband, as he is the head of the household. My husband and I would laugh behind my mom's back over comments like that because my mom thought some duties were supposed to be performed by women and not by men or the other way around. With time, I realized that my mom somehow became aware of the Western world culture and how things work in the Western world. Sometimes, she commented, "I am not sure, my daughter, how you manage to take care of your kids, go to school, and work full time."

Speaking about the Western world and culture, I will not forget the grief I received from my mom after taking her to the doctor for a mammogram and pap smear. These forms of health screening and maintenance were all new to my mom. This was my mom's first time going through those health screenings. She would not stop complaining about how the mammogram machine squeezed her breast so hard. I remember giving her some analgesics afterward. I was happy to have my mom screened for breast and cervical cancer; both exams came back normal.

Another experience I will not forget is when my mom visited us and went with her for antenatal appointments when I was pregnant with our second daughter, Ify. My mom enjoyed going with me to those doctors' appointments. I will never forget when the technician drew blood; my mom would complain afterward about why I should not let them draw so much blood from me since I was carrying a baby. She did not think it would be healthy for the baby. She assumed they were drawing a lot of blood from me. I get a kick each time I think about it and my mom. Another thing that makes me laugh each time I remember the incident was when my mom visited us at the hospital when I had my second child (Ify). She would not carry our child until we gave her money. Growing up, it was traditional to give grandmas money when they saw their grandchildren for the first time and carried their grandkids. I watched my sisters give my mom money the first time she carried their children. I could not get over my husband's reaction and tried to explain the tradition to my husband.

I could tell that my mother was particularly proud to take care of her granddaughter (Mojo). She braided her hair and fed her all kinds of African food. To this day, my oldest daughter enjoys eating African foods more than her siblings, and periodically, she wants me to make African foods, especially Fufu, with the traditional soup. Fufu (or foo foo or fou fou) is one of the most famous West African "swallow" foods. It is a filling side dish- starchy, smooth, dense, and stretchy. There are so many versions of Fufu. It can come from cassava, yam, oat, or plantain. It is beloved because it is delicious, especially when you swallow it with a lovely African soup such as melon, okra, or other African soup. It is satisfying and easy to prepare. For any West African gathering or occasion, having fufu and soup is essential, just as jollof rice and other meat such as goat meat. It is funny that my daughter always comments, "Thanks to grandma for teaching me how to eat African food." My mom spent almost two years with us in the United States and left two months after we had our second daughter (Ify). I still remember the agony I felt when my mom left us. It was after Ify was baptized. We came home, celebrated, and took my mom to the airport. But I appreciated all her help and support when she visited us.

This picture was taken after a church service
when Mom visited the United States.

Another picture of my mom when she visited
the United States.

With mom and Mojo after a Church Service in
the United States.

Mom with Mojo after a Church Service in the
United States.

With mom after a Church Service in the
United States.

With mom and Mojo after a Church Service in
the United States. On this day, Mojo took her
first walk. It was a joy to watch Mojo walk for
the first time. My mom had been practicing
walking with Mojo. My mom was so happy to
see Mojo take her first few steps. My mother
was so happy with Mojo's accomplishment. I
was pregnant with Ify. Mom was finally getting
used to spending time in the United States.

With mom during Mojo's Baptism in the United States.

This was during Ify's baptism. Ify was barely two months old. This is the final picture we took with Mom. Mom could finally attend a church service without wearing a head scarf. Mom was wearing a black-and-white dress. She left for Nigeria on this day.

CHAPTER 11

When My Mom Got Sick

My mom left the United States in October 2000, after I gave birth to my second child. I remember vividly that she left on October 20, when my second daughter was baptized. I wanted her to stay with us longer, but she said she had to go home to care for my stepsisters and brother. My second child was less than two months old, and I was pursuing my master's degree with two young kids. My oldest child was barely a year old then. It was such a sad moment after seeing her off at the airport.

After returning home, my mom got busy raising my stepsiblings. She embarked on her old business of selling palm oil and farming on our lands. She worked tirelessly to provide for all the kids and took a particular liking for my brother. She ensured all the kids got a high school education and were trained in a trade.

In 2006, I was told my mom complained about one of her toes having what seemed like a fungal infection. Initially, it seemed harmless and appeared to be responding to treatment. I sent her money so she would go to the hospital to be seen by a doctor. I was told her toe felt better afterward. The infection spread to other toes and beyond shortly after that. It became so infected that I had to send dressing materials from the United States to care for the wound. I remember paying some nurses to care for her wound dressing at home. For some reason, my mom started having problems walking and would find it difficult to get around because of the pain in her foot.

That foot, from what I was told by the doctor that I paid to examine her, had gotten gangrenous, and he recommended partial amputation. There was a lot of family misunderstanding on how to handle her condition. Some family members resorted to using the money I sent for my mother's care to seek the services of a native healer who would use all kinds of dirt in the name of traditional medicine on the wound. Before too long, the wound had spread beyond the foot and had gone to the ankle area. I pleaded with my family members to take her to the hospital, to no avail. The situation got so bad that my mom had so much pain without reasonable pain control. It was such a trying moment that I lost weight and cried almost every day, mainly when I listened to my mom on the phone as she moaned in pain and did not have anyone to listen to my recommendations about my mother's care. It was such a challenging time that the family dynamic was at an all-time low.

After some time, my mom could not take it and decided she would like to go to the hospital. By then, the wound had spread beyond the ankle with massive pain. When my mom finally got to the hospital, the surgeon decided that my mom needed a below-the-knee amputation. The surgery went as planned. My mom spent at least three weeks at the hospital. While getting ready to be discharged from the hospital, she started having the same problem on the other foot, leading to another below-the-knee amputation. My mother endured two major surgeries in less than two months without complications. And through it all, I had to cover all the hospital expenses without help from other family members.

After the hospital stay, my mom, who had been active all her life, was now a double amputee. She now needed help with all her daily living activities. Through it all, she was nice about it and would not complain. When I visited home in 2008, I could tell she was more disappointed about not being able to go to the farm or care for her family than losing both legs. My mom tried to live her life as normally as she could. I bought her a wheelchair, even artificial limbs she sometimes used when she went around, and things around her house that would help her. At one time, I had traveled with commodes from the United States. I tried to make her life as easy as possible, considering her immense disability. I even suggested she visit the United States to seek care, but she refused. Despite all the difficulties, she attended church and other community activities as usual. She would attend all the local meetings and visit her friends without a problem.

CHAPTER 12

My Mom Later Years and Death

A couple of years later, my mother had a stroke. My mom had always been healthy, but because she was in one place and unable to do things she used to, her pressure started increasing, and she had a stroke. Initially, she recovered some bodily functions, like moving her arms and trying to feed herself. Her speech was greatly affected, and she never regained her speech well. Not too long after that, she had another stroke.

This time, it was worse than the initial one. Her speech worsened until you barely understood her when she spoke. I realized later that family members entrusted in her care and to whom I was sending money to care for our mom provided suboptimal care.

Through it all, my mother kept her faith up. She still went to church whenever she could. The priest would sometimes come to the house to offer her Holy Communion and would bless her. Since 2008, I have had to visit home almost yearly to care for her. I took home medical supplies, including medications and everything she needed. Periodically, she would end up in the hospital for several days and feel well afterward. I would say that since 2015, her condition got worse. She was experiencing more difficulty swallowing food and spitting. By mid-July 2015, my mom's condition worsened. During this time, she was aphasic and could not talk for three weeks. Everybody in my household thought my mom was nearing the end of her time on earth. I will not forget one early morning in July when my bother Chimaobi woke me up and told me that our mom was talking and wanted to talk to me. I barely understood her, and she asked if I was planning to visit home in December or Christmas.

I asked her if she would want me to visit home, and she said yes. After speaking with her, I bought my plane ticket to visit home in December. When the time came, I traveled home and spent approximately three weeks. It was the best time I had with my mom. I slept in the same bed with her and took care of all her needs, including taking her to the hospital for care. Most evenings, my mom would have conversations with me. Most conversations centered around her last wishes on earth. One thing that was so dear to my mom was ensuring my brother and his family were cared for when she was gone. She wanted to ensure my brother was mentored and supported while she was gone. During our conversations, she placed her right hand on my left chest and made me promise to take care of my brother and his family. I turned around and placed my right hand on her left upper chest and promised her that I would care for my brother and my extended family when she was gone. I could see the relief on her face afterward.

On the day I left for the United States, we both cried, knowing that this was probably the last time we would see each other again while my mom was alive. I remember removing my necklace with Rosary beads and putting it on my mom's neck. I was happy that when my mom passed away, she was still wearing the necklace I had given her the last time I was home. My last visit was in December 2015, and I left in January 2016. During the same year, my mom got sicker, suffered heart failure, and passed away on September 29, 2016. I will never forget that day, approximately four in the evening, United States time. I was heartbroken listening to her on the cellphone speaker as she took her last breath.

My mother was survived by ten children, 30 grandchildren, and 33 great-grandchildren. She was also survived by her only surviving sibling, Auntie Utemma, who was then in Canada with her children and was absent from her sister's funeral due to complex logistics.

After our mom came back from the United States with my eldest sister, Daa Rose.

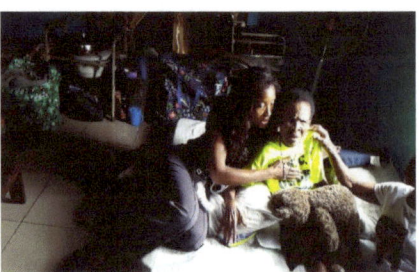

The last picture I took with my mom was in January 2016. The day I came back to the United States after spending approximately three weeks with Mom.

Some of the grandkids are at Mom's burial graveside.

One year of my mom's death-picture taken when I went home for my mom's memorial service in December 2017. At mom's graveside.

CHAPTER 13

Specific Life Lessons from My Mother

As a child, my mother taught me how important it is to worship God with your heart and soul. My mother introduced me to God early on in life. She would wake me up as young as maybe five, early in the morning to attend the morning Rosary and mass before going to school. In addition, she influenced me to attend church services not only on Sundays but on the holy days of obligation. Growing up, we attended mass on Sundays and other days of obligation. She would make sure we went for evening Sunday benedictions. She made sure we attended reconciliations at least every two weeks.

My mom taught me that giving is always better than receiving. Volunteerism was essential to my mother. She volunteered in church a lot. She would sometimes go to church early in the morning to clean the church. She would organize the women in our compound to clean the main roads leading to my family's big compound. She would organize them to make sure every one of them did their civic duties to the community, state, and federal government. She would galvanize my family members on election days to get out and vote. She belonged to different religious organizations and volunteered her time.

My mother was forgiving and compassionate. She forgave every one of my evil uncles who was mean to her. She always helped each of them and their spouses. When some passed away, she was there for their widows and supported them. She would feed their children when they visited our house. I marveled and was sometimes surprised at the level of forgiveness and respect she would give to some of my wicked uncles.

My mother never discriminated. Our house is by the roadside, and the door is always open. Anybody inside the house is guaranteed to be received by my mother. I have witnessed her feeding the homeless and the mentally ill who would walk inside the house. She would let anyone who walked inside the house sit at the same dinner table with us during meals. Sometimes, she would cook extra for some members of my compound, like older people, who needed help and could not afford to cook for themselves.

I learned the importance of sticking with and loving your family members regardless of the situation. My mother loved her mother and siblings. My grandmother refused to move in with any of her children and instead would visit her children periodically. While in elementary school, my mother ensured we visited our grandmother every weekend. I took a particular interest in my grandmother and would stay at her home with my cousin (Ahunna) every Friday after school to spend weekends with our grandmother. My mother loved her siblings and would ensure they ate and gave them gifts whenever they visited our house. She was respectful to her oldest sister, who passed away a couple of years before my mother. My mother loved her two brothers and would give them gifts periodically. My mother loved her younger sister, Auntie Utemma, and was always nice to her and her children.

My mom was so happy when I got accepted at
the Alvan Ikoku College of Education-Nigeria.

The picture was taken during my
matriculation at Alvan Ikoku College of
Education in Owerri-Imo State-Nigeria.

CHAPTER 14

Final Thoughts

September 29, 2024, will be eight years since my mom died at the age of 91 years old. Throughout these years and as I get older, I begin to appreciate my mother not only as my mom but as a role model. It has been challenging to navigate life without contacting my mom. I will forever cherish all that she did for me and my siblings. I appreciate her advice and how she lived an exemplary and simple life. I am forever indebted to her and proud and happy to call her my beloved mom and role model.

I am happy to share a few of the words I shared during my mom's funeral. I appreciate your reading this memoir and hope you learn one or two things from it.

CHAPTER 15

A Tribute to My Wonderful Mother

My beautiful mom! You are my inspiration and role model. I love you so much, and death will never destroy my love for you. You laid a good foundation for your children and me in particular. You beat all odds as you single-handedly raised your children with grace and candor. Despite the adversities you faced, you never for once complained. I learned a lot from you, my precious mom! You taught me the value of hard work, perseverance, honesty, and, most importantly, God's love and infinite mercy. I am who I am today because of you. You encouraged me to reach for the skies and do my best.

You embodied these words from George Washington, the United States' first President, "My mother was the most beautiful woman I ever saw. All I am, I owe my mother. I attribute all my success in life to the moral, intellectual, and physical education I received from her." No words can express the ache I feel because of your absence. You left an indelible mark on your children, especially me. I am now passing on your teachings and the values you ingrained in me to my children. I always looked forward to each telephone conversation; I miss hearing your particular pet name for me, "NneNwokorieche," that you passionately called me. Mother, you worked hard; I hope you enjoy reuniting with our loved ones, especially your loving husband. As you always told us, "that the Holy Spirit revealed to you that on your last day on earth, the Angels will join you in a feast filled with pomp and pageantry," I have no doubt you have joined your Creator. So, my dearest, sweet, loving mom, I LOVE you now and forever! Rest in the bosom of the Lord until we meet again to part no more...Amen.

CHAPTER 16

A Special Poem for My Mother

When I think of my mom,
I think of a woman I am proud to call my mom.
She has been with me throughout my life,
Watching me grow the way God made me.
Sometimes, I falter, but she is always there to guide and lift me.
When I think of my mom,
I think of a strong, God-fearing, and honest woman.
She loves God so much and never loses faith in God.
When I think of my mom,
I think of a wife who fought hard to maintain her husband's legacy.
When I think of my mom,
I think of her tender love toward her children, grandchildren, and
great-grandchildren.
When I think of my mom,
I think of a woman who never felt sorry for herself:
A woman of grace and gentleness,
A woman who forgave those who did her wrong.
When I think of my mom,
I think of a woman who taught me like no other.

And I am thankful; I am the lucky one.

I had the opportunity to call her my mom.

About The Author

Ngozi Mbue, Ph.D., APRN, ANP-C, is an educator, nurse scientist, inventor, and clinician living with her family in Houston, Texas. She likes reading books, cooking, and visiting her family and friends abroad in her spare time.

ACKNOWLEDGEMENTS

I am incredibly grateful to my mother, who taught me how to love and forgive, among other things. She inspired me by the way she lived her life. I am grateful to my sisters, brother, Auntie Utemma, my cousins, especially Mrs. Ahunna Iwueze, and extended family members. I am also grateful to my husband, John, and my wonderful children, Mojoko (Mojo), Ifeoma (Ify), and Ilome. I offer an extra thank you and appreciate Ms. Otilia Sanchez, who assisted in editing this book. I will always cherish my dad for his vision, aspirations, and his special love for his family.

www.ingramcontent.com/pod-product-compliance
Lightning Source LLC
Chambersburg PA
CBHW040847120626
46547CB00001B/70